The Tao *of* Happiness

莊子之道

JEREMY P. TARCHER / PENGUIN

an imprint of Penguin Random House

New York

The Tao *of* Happiness

Stories from Chuang Tzu for Your Spiritual Journey

DEREK LIN

JEREMY P. TARCHER/PENGUIN
An imprint of Penguin Random House LLC
375 Hudson Street
New York, New York 10014

Most Tarcher/Penguin books are available at special quantity discounts for bulk purchase for sales promotions, premiums, fund-raising, and educational needs. Special books or book excerpts also can be created to fit specific needs. For details, write: SpecialMarkets@penguinrandomhouse.com.

Library of Congress Cataloging-in-Publication Data
Lin, Derek. 1964– author.
The Tao of happiness : stories from Chuang Tzu for your spiritual journey / Derek Lin.
pages cm
ISBN 978-0-399-17551-0
1. Tao.   2. Taoism.   3. Spiritual life—Taoism.   4. Zhuangzi.   I. Title.
B127.T3L56 2015
299.5'1482—dc23
2015024087

Printed in the United States of America
1 3 5 7 9 10 8 6 4 2

BOOK DESIGN BY NICOLE LAROCHE

Contents

Introduction

莊子之道

If you have not encountered Chuang Tzu before, you are in for a treat. He was the sage who stood apart from all others in Chinese history. He was a unique presence, a great mind like no one before or since.

If you have encountered Chuang Tzu before in other books, you may find that this book offers a different approach by focusing on his stories, rather than on historical footnotes or scholarly citations. In Chinese culture, Chuang Tzu is not an academic subject to be analyzed but a source of inspiration and insight.

The name "Chuang Tzu" ("Zhuangzi" in the Pinyin system) means Master Chuang. His full name was Chuang Chou (Zhuang Zhou), and he lived about twenty-four hundred years ago, during the Warring States period. It was a time of death and destruction due to widespread warfare. It was also a time when many schools of philosophy emerged, perhaps as a response to the extreme chaos.

Chuang Tzu quickly distinguished himself and became well known for his deep understanding and sense of humor. His mastery was such that he could explain the Tao with simple stories. His humor was such that he could see the joy in ordinary things. He taught his students about "carefree wandering"—the path of moving through life with a free and happy heart, regardless of how turbulent the journey might be. He regarded this as the Tao of true happiness.

His teachings were collected in the classic known as *Nan Hua Ching* (*Nan Hua Jing*), and it had a tremendous impact on Chinese culture. Many common sayings and expressions in modern Mandarin trace directly back to it. The concepts and ideas within its pages are actively studied and appreciated today. As long as Chinese culture lives, the legacy of Chuang Tzu will also endure.

It is time for us to join in on the fun. Chuang Tzu's wisdom is not just for the Chinese, but for all humanity. We may not have the instability or the clash of massive armies in the Warring States period, but we definitely have a lot of stress and tension in these modern times. Many of us find ourselves fighting little battles on the personal front just to get through the day. We can definitely benefit greatly from Chuang Tzu's teachings.

The best way for us to learn also happens to be the easiest. Chuang Tzu loved to teach through stories. The tales he crafted drew his students in, captured their imagination, and conveyed the Tao in unforgettable ways.

As you take in the stories, you will see that Chuang Tzu had a unique perspective on just about everything. He rejected conventional concepts. He took numerous notions to a level beyond the mundane to reveal how different things looked in the Tao. When people mourned the death of a loved one, he showed them that it made more sense to celebrate a life well lived. When philosophers talked about living with no particular goals or traveling with no particular destinations, he described the spiritual journey as the sacred quest for the Tao*—a journey full of meaning, undertaken with definite direction and purpose.

This spiritual journey is exactly what we will delve into with this book. It is the great truth behind Chuang Tzu's idea of carefree wandering. It is also his ultimate teaching, where the process of learning about the journey is a journey in its own right.

So . . . what is the nature of Chuang Tzu's spiritual journey, and how do we prepare for it? What are the challenges along the way? How do we get the most out of the trip? What happens when we get to the destination? Let us begin by asking these questions . . . and let the stories of Chuang Tzu bring us the best answers.

---

* All *Tao Te Ching* translations quoted herein are from the author's original work published in 2006 as *Tao Te Ching: Annotated and Explained*.

PART 1

Departure

Before we embark on the spiritual journey, we should take some time to contemplate the journey itself. Tao sages always know what they are getting into and never rush into anything blindly. Let us emulate them by understanding the nature of the journey and mentally preparing ourselves:

1. Chuang Tzu likens the spiritual journey to the long flight of a giant bird high in the sky. This flight can be seen as the lifelong path of Tao cultivation, the quest of learning and exploration, and the sacred task that you are in this world to accomplish.

2. Be ready for the mind-expanding effect of the Tao. The teachings of Chuang Tzu will show you a whole new world and open up your spiritual dimensions dramatically. Once you are immersed in this vast ocean of wisdom, you will not be able to go back to the more limited perspective.

3. There may be those who denigrate your efforts as useless. When dealing with such people, hold on to the thought that your path is unique, just as you are unique. Nothing is absolutely useless in the Tao, and your journey will prove to be supremely useful, for it will enable you to change your world. This change is a gift that only you can bring.

4. The outcome of your journey will, to a large degree, depend on how you use the Tao. Some will use it only for philosophical discussions or playing with ideas, but you must go far beyond that level. Use the Tao to do great work and propel yourself to go the distance. The Tao is unlimited—do not limit yourself when you tap into it.

The Flight of the Peng Bird

鵬程萬里

In the Northern Sea, there is a giant fish. Its name is Kun. Its size is incredibly large. No one knows how many thousands of miles its length measures.

The Kun fish is able to transform into a bird, known as Peng. The Peng bird is also incredibly large. No one knows how many thousands of miles its wingspan measures.

When the Peng bird flies with all its might, its wings are like the clouds that hang from the sky. This massive bird migrates to the Southern Sea when great winds blow across the ocean. The Southern Sea, its destination, is also known as the Heavenly Pond.

An ancient chronicle of strange phenomena describes it this way: "When the Peng bird begins its flight to the Southern Sea, it splashes water from the surface of the ocean for thousands of miles. Its wings generate a hurricane force to lift it up to a height of ninety thousand miles. This occurs in the month of June, when the wind is at its strongest."

When the Peng bird flies, it can be seen from afar. This is similar to how one sees wild horses running and kicking up a cloud of dust from a distance. All living things move in accordance with nature, just as nature moves in accordance with all living things.

A cicada and a turtledove look up to see the Peng bird in the sky. They find the whole idea of the journey ludicrous. The turtledove laughs in mockery: "I fly with all my strength and stop when I get to a tree. Sometimes I can't even make it that far so I drop to the ground. Why would anyone bother flying ninety thousand miles to wherever?"

From the Peng bird's position beyond the clouds, it sees the true color of the sky and the unlimited expanse of heaven. When the Peng bird looks down, it sees everything below fading into the hazy distance. Lifted by powerful winds beneath its giant wings, the Peng bird pays no heed to ground-level chatter. It directs its attention to the horizon and continues its flight toward the Southern Sea.

The Tao

In the Chinese-speaking parts of the world, "*peng cheng wan li*" is the most frequently used expression in graduation ceremonies. It is the equivalent of "go forth" in the West, and its meaning is similar: May you go far in life, live up to your potential, and achieve great things.

Peng cheng wan li can be roughly translated as "the giant Peng bird travels ten thousand miles." It is a direct reference to this story, where the flight of the Peng bird is the metaphor for a journey of great achievement. Chuang Tzu's original purpose in writing this story was not to inspire high school or university graduates. He wrote it for everyone. The inspiration he expressed was intended for all human beings.

In life, you start out as the Kun fish. The great size of the Kun fish is the vast potential within you. You already possess all the power you need to become the Peng bird, but that power has to be activated. Prior to the activation, your potential remains dormant, and you continue day after day in the cold depths of the Northern Sea, swimming around and not really getting anywhere.

To activate or awaken the power within, you must answer the calling for something greater than yourself. In the story, the calling manifests as the great winds blowing across the ocean. You respond to such a calling by making a definite decision to commit yourself. This commitment may be to a cause you believe in, or a personal goal to do your best in contributing more to the world. Whatever the specifics may be, your decision is what triggers the transformation. You become the Peng bird, rising quickly out of the depths, shooting up to the clouds and beyond. Nothing can stop you.

The meaning of the story is as clear as can be to the Chinese, but in the West it is not quite as clear. There may be Western students of the Tao who feel that having a goal or destination is not in keeping with the free-flowing nature of the Tao. Some may argue that goal-setting is a trap that leads to strain and strife. To them, the flight of the Peng bird is inconsistent with Chuang Tzu's concept of carefree wandering.

To clear up this misunderstanding, we only need to realize that being carefree does not preclude having a goal or destination. The reverse is also true—having a goal or destination does not prevent you from feeling carefree. This is because carefree wandering does not mean aimless wandering. In fact, knowing where you are going and how to get there will do wonders to remove any uncertainty and anxiety from your mind. This lets you relax and enjoy the process of getting there. Having clarity on your goal or destination is what makes the carefree state of mind possible.

You may know people who already have this kind of clarity in life. If so, observe how they speak with confidence and take actions with definite purpose. They exude happiness because they've been liberated from the pain of an empty and meaningless existence. They radiate joy because they can see themselves getting closer to the fulfillment of their dreams. Is it any surprise that these are the people who "go forth" feeling absolutely carefree?

You can be at that level too. You can embody both the Peng bird and the carefree wandering in the recognition that there is no contradiction between the two. It all starts with knowing the purpose to which you must commit yourself. If you already know your mission in life, this part requires only a simple decision to proceed. If you do not yet feel that level of certainty, set for yourself the goal of lifelong cultivation until something more definite comes along. Either way, everything will start falling into place as you transform from the Kun to the Peng for the long flight. This marks the beginning of your spiritual journey, your own path on the Tao of Happiness.

You may encounter naysayers as you make your preparations. They don't have any ideas of their own, but that won't stop them from commenting that your ideas won't work. They may know very little about you or your spiritual interests, but that won't stop them from expressing disdain or disapproval. Like the cicada and the turtledove, they are capable of only short, limited trips. They have no idea what it means to prepare for a lifelong journey that is as majestic as it is spiritual.

Through this story, Chuang Tzu is telling us how to deal with them. The Peng bird is so high up in the stratosphere that it cannot hear any of the noises from the ground. Similarly, when you elevate yourself to greater heights, negative people will no longer get under your skin. If that is not the case—if you still find yourself bothered by the cicadas and turtledoves of the world—it can only be because you are still too close to their level. You must go higher. You must raise the bar in your mind by making your goal grander, or by switching to a goal that really fires you up. When the negativity no longer affects you, you will know that you have reached cruising altitude.

Do not feel obligated to lower yourself in order to engage the negativity. You do not owe anyone an explanation. The gap between you and the naysayers is so great that nothing can bridge it. The best thing you can do is to let go of the need to debate or argue and simply move on. Let your view of them fade into the hazy distance as you climb higher. Direct your attention to the horizon, and continue your flight toward the Southern Sea. It is your destination . . . as well as your destiny.

The Frog in the Well

井底之蛙

Once upon a time *in ancient China, there was a frog who lived in an abandoned well. He considered himself the master of his domain and felt quite satisfied with it.*

One day, he saw a sea turtle moving slowly nearby. He felt like some conversation to liven up an otherwise boring day, so he called out a greeting. The sea turtle approached to return the greeting. Upon seeing the frog's smug expression, he said, "You seem happy. That is good."

"Happy? Of course I am happy!" The frog smiled proudly. "Look at my life! Whenever I want, I can hop around the outside of this well. When I feel tired, I can go inside the well to rest. Sometimes I enjoy the water, so I go soaking in it. Sometimes I enjoy the mud, so I run my feet through it." He pointed at the smaller crea-

tures in the well. "See the tadpoles and the others? They cannot compare to me. I know more than they do. I enjoy life more than they can imagine. This well is my territory, and I own the water. This is as good as it gets!"

The sea turtle did not respond, but the frog was in a generous mood, so he offered: "Why don't you come into the well and take a look? I want you to see for yourself."

The frog jumped into the well and the sea turtle tried to follow, but even before he could get his left foot in the well, his right foot was already stuck. There was no way he could fit through, so he backed away. "I am sorry," he said to the frog, "your well may be a bit small for me."

"Small?" The frog did not understand. "It is not small. It has more space than I will ever need. It is big. Big! Do you even know what 'big' means?"

The sea turtle was amused by the question. "Well, I come from the ocean, and I know the ocean is truly big."

"Is that right?" The frog got defensive. "What are we talking about exactly? Twice as big as my well? Three times as big? Is that what you mean?"

The sea turtle shook his head. "We cannot really describe the ocean in those terms. It is larger than we can measure with a thousand miles, and deeper than we can measure with a thousand yards."

The frog was confused. He could not imagine anything that spanned a thousand miles, much less something that went beyond such measurements. Upon seeing his confusion, the sea turtle knew he had to explain it in a different way.

He said: "There was a time in the distant past when we had nine years of continuous downpour and floods, but the ocean did not increase in size. There was also another time when we had seven years of continuous drought, but the ocean did not shrink, either. You see, the ocean is so big that even such drastic changes in the weather over long periods of time did not affect it one way or another."

This finally got through to the frog. He was shocked as his mind struggled to grasp it. How could something that big exist?

The sea turtle continued: "There is happiness in such a place, just as there is in your well. Perhaps we can call it the great happiness of the limitless ocean."

The sea turtle sensed he had said enough. The frog was still staring at him, completely speechless. The sea turtle bid him farewell. It was time for him to resume his journey.

The Tao

"*Jing di zhi wa*" is one of the most common expressions in Chinese. It can be translated as "the frog at the bottom of the well," which describes someone who has such a limited perspective that he is ignorant of his ignorance. The expression comes directly from this story, in which the frog is diametrically opposite to the Peng bird in the previous story.

The usefulness of the story goes beyond the expression. It asks the following questions:

- What are you? Are you the tadpole, the frog, or the sea turtle?
- Where are you? Are you in the abandoned well or the limitless ocean?

The tadpole is the person who has little or no understanding of spiritual matters. He never looks beyond the physical to ponder the deeper questions of life, like the tadpole never venturing outside the well. He may not even realize there is anything that needs exploring.

The frog is someone who becomes full of himself upon gaining a little knowledge. He knows a bit about the Tao—not as much as he imagines, but enough to make him feel superior to the tadpole. His illusion of superiority gives him a feeling of happiness that is also illusory.

The sea turtle is a Tao cultivator who applies the teachings to life. Such a cultivator is immersed in the great Tao, like the sea turtle living in the ocean, and has direct experience of its vastness. The sea turtle is a worthy aspiration for all of us.

The difference between the frog and the sea turtle comes from what they learn. The limited understanding of the frog is similar to academic trivia and esoteric distinctions. This kind of knowledge has no impact on one's life and zero practical value, and it gives rise to arrogance. A frog in our world would be someone who can rattle off definitions of specialized terms, not realizing that his ivory tower can in fact be an abandoned well, and the water in it is stagnant and stale.

In the ocean, the sea turtle is surrounded by unlimited wisdom. In our world, this wisdom manifests as Tao teachings about connections and relationships. It is a practical path of spirituality that impacts every aspect of one's life, and its greatness inspires humility. The sea turtle lives in gratitude for the ocean, which is not only vast but also dynamic. Everything in it is always different, and always interesting.

The well is finite—the ocean is infinite. No matter how you multiply a finite quantity, the result is still finite. On the other hand, no matter how you add to or subtract from the infinite, you still get infinity. One cannot compare the measurable water of the well to the immeasurable water of the ocean, just as one cannot compare the illusory happiness of the frog in the well to the authentic happiness of the Tao.

If you are the frog who's been hopping around the well, it is time to stop and join the sea turtle. Instead of comparing yourself with people who don't know much about the Tao, look to experienced cultivators as examples to inspire you. See how they immerse themselves in the Tao, and consider the same approach for yourself.

If you are the sea turtle who's been interrupted while heading for the ocean, it is time to continue on your way. As much as you want to share the Tao, there is only so much you can do for those who are unable to understand. Extend an invitation for them to join you whenever they are ready, and resume your journey. The vast ocean of the Tao is waiting for you.

Useful and Useless

有用無用

One day, Chuang Tzu *and his friend Hui Tzu were having a discussion about the Tao. At one point, in disagreeing with Chuang Tzu, Hui Tzu said: "Suppose I have this big tree called the Shu tree. Its trunk is all twisted lumps and knotty bumps; its branches are all bent and crooked. It has no straight runs anywhere that can be used as timber, so carpenters and builders pass by without a second look. What you are talking about now is just like that tree—ideas that are big but useless. That's why people ignore you."*

Sensing the challenge in his friend's words, Chuang Tzu smiled. "Hui Tzu, have you seen wildcats and foxes? They are certainly not big, and they seem quite useful as they jump this way and that. They may move around with great speed and agility, but then they fall into a trap and die in the hunter's net. Compare them to the bison, this huge animal with a body that seems as big as a cloud in the sky. It cannot catch mice like cats can, but its strength is far beyond anything smaller creatures can muster.

"This big Shu tree is no different. You consider it useless, but think about what happens when you plant such a tree in an empty field. Everyone will come to enjoy its shade and rest freely under its shelter. As you have pointed out, no one will ever chop it down, so it will always be around. It is precisely because it is useless that it will never be harmed. In other words, its uselessness turns out to be its greatest usefulness!"

The Tao

This story highlights the difference between the conventional thinking of the typical person and the unconventional thinking of the Tao cultivator. Many people don't really "get" the Tao because they see only the surface appearance. Those who cultivate the Tao look beyond the superficial for insights that are not immediately apparent.

1. *Spirituality*
   When this teaching is applied to spirituality, the Shu tree is an apt metaphor for the Tao. It cannot be used in the conventional sense, so people dismiss it as being of no value at all. This parallels the situation in our world, where the Tao is often regarded as not much more than a quaint and exotic notion. People have vague ideas that it has something to do with Buddhism and meditation, but what is it, exactly? *Can I use it when I go to church on Sundays? Will it make me look more pious to my peers? If not, then this so-called Tao is useless to me, and I am not interested.*

   Chuang Tzu does not necessarily see the lack of popularity as a disadvantage. If no one wants to use the tree in the conventional sense, then that also means no one will come around to disturb the peace. This is why it does not matter to Tao cultivators that their way of life is not as well known as mainstream religions. The lack of popularity can be a good thing in that no one will use the Tao as their justification for extremism. No wars will be waged over the Tao, no acts of violence or oppression will be carried out in its name.

This does not imply any sort of weakness in the Tao. Tao cultivators are like the bison. They do not engage in frantic activities like wildcats and foxes. They have no missionary zeal that drives them to proselytize everywhere. They are content to be connected to the power of the Tao without trying to show it off to anyone. Theirs is a quiet strength beyond the understanding of the conventional mind.

2. *Society*

When this teaching is applied to society, it gives rise to "planting trees" as a recurring theme in Chinese culture. It means creating something worthwhile that withstands the test of time and brings great benefits to all. The tree may begin as a sapling, but in time it grows big enough for many people. It not only provides comfort and protection under its shade but also becomes a focal point for a community. People meet at the tree to converse, make plans, or just hang out and enjoy one another's company.

Tao cultivators are inspired by this idea to plant trees of their own. This can happen in many different aspects of life and may not involve actual trees or any plants at all. It can be anything, from building a library to promote literacy, to paving a road to ease transportation, to living a life with total integrity to serve as an example for others. Whenever Tao cultivators see an empty field—an aspect of life that can benefit from the Tao—they think about what they can do to plant the seed.

This is the perfect story to reference when people question your personal path. They may not understand you, and the Tao may seem rather useless to them, but that is only to be expected. Its seeming uselessness, like the Shu tree, is the secret that hides its true usefulness.

3. *Humanity*

When this teaching is applied to us, it tells us that no one is truly useless. The Shu tree is like the quiet kids, the loners who cannot hope to compete with the popular kids who are cool or good-looking or athletic and therefore "useful" for everything from sports to social activities. The misfits are the ones who get picked on, laughed at, excluded, and ignored, since they are completely "useless" for anything.

Chuang Tzu points out that the truth is more than meets the eyes. These kids learn to deal with setbacks and solitude. They develop their internal resources. They come up with better plans for the future. Before you know it, the ugly duckling has become the beautiful swan; the class geek has become classy and chic; the nerd has become the celebrated inventor or entrepreneur. The "useless" tree turns out to be quite useful indeed, and the misfits have grown up to be distinguished individuals.

Do you see the Shu tree in someone? If so, then treat that person with kindness and respect. Be different from all the ignorant ones who taunt or bully or play cruel jokes. Be the friend that no one else wants to be. In time, you will see how right you are in following the Tao, and in nurturing the hidden greatness of others.

Do you see the Shu tree in yourself? If so, then take it from Chuang Tzu that you are not as useless as the mundane world would have you believe. A grand destiny like the flight of the Peng bird is not reserved for the jock or the class president or the prom queen alone. It is meant for you.

The greatest Shu tree of all is the one in your heart, where your spirit can rest under its shade. It is the source of your ideas to make the world a better place and the wellspring of your compassion for all fellow human beings. It is also the driving force for your spiritual quest—a pursuit that many would say is useless. Their opinions do not matter to you, for you alone know the truth. The "useless" Tao is a power far beyond anything small minds can imagine . . . and you are just beginning to explore the infinite ways it can be used.

Secret Formula

宋人的秘方

Once upon a time *in ancient China, there was a family in the Song Kingdom known for being in the cloth-bleaching business for many generations. Every day, the family workers soaked textiles in a special bleaching solution and then took them into the river to let the flowing currents wash away the bleach. Old clothes and bedsheets ended up looking as good as new.*

When winter came around, most businesses that depended on the river would close for the season. The weather would get so cold and dry that wading into the river would cause the skin to split into painful cracks, thus making work impossible. This family was the exception to the rule, because they had a special ointment to protect their hands. This ointment was made from a secret formula passed down through the generations, and it allowed them to work through wintertime.

One day, a traveler who had heard about the ointment came to visit the family. He offered to buy the secret formula for a hundred gold pieces. The head of the family was amazed by this offer. Normally, it would take him decades to save up that much money.

He discussed it with family members: "We've been working in this cloth-bleaching business for generations, and we can barely make ends meet. Now we only need to sell the formula and we'll get a hundred gold pieces. Surely it cannot get any better than this!" He looked around the room and saw that everyone was nodding in agreement. It was a deal.

The transaction took place. The money changed hands; the cloth bleacher brought out the secret formula and made a careful copy. The traveler went on his way, and life returned to normal for the family.

The traveler went to the palace of King Wu and sought an audience. In the royal chambers, he presented the secret formula and explained how to produce massive quantities for the king's army. King Wu had been at war with the neighboring Yue Kingdom for many years but could never gain the upper hand. Now, with his entire army using the ointment, he launched the first winter offensive ever in the history of the two kingdoms.

The armies clashed over the bordering river. The ointment worked as expected and protected Wu soldiers, while Yue soldiers lacked this protection and were fully exposed to the elements. After only a few days, many Yue soldiers developed such painful cracks that they could not even hold their weapons. Soon, King Wu deci-mated the Yue army and unified the two territories under his rule.

In gratitude to the traveler who played such a pivotal role in his victory, King Wu granted him a large estate and made him a noble. As the traveler settled into his new, privileged life, he reflected on the path that took him there. Endless wealth was his, acquired with the secret formula for only a hundred gold pieces. Surely, he thought, it could not get any better than this!

The Tao

In this story, the ointment represents the Tao. Just as the secret formula was passed down from generation to generation, so too are the teachings of the Tao. Today, many people are still not aware of these teachings, so a genuine tradition of the Tao remains something of a well-kept secret in the modern world.

As the story shows, the ointment can be used in different ways, but no matter how it is used, its formula is the same. The Tao is similar in that it can also be used in different ways, but no matter how you use it, it is still the Tao. The dramatic difference in results is created by the person using it.

Some people regard the Tao as a philosophical pastime or an academic pursuit. Using the Tao this way is like using the ointment for cloth bleaching. There is nothing wrong with it, but there is definitely a lot of untapped potential in this scenario. The better way to use the Tao is to go beyond intellectuality and apply it as a way of life. This is like the traveler's way of using the ointment— much more powerful than the way of the cloth bleacher.

The king or emperor in a Tao story is usually a reference to you. The absolute power that such a ruler wields is a reference to the absolute power you possess over yourself. Thus, the traveler's advice for King Wu is in fact Chuang

Tzu's instruction for you. In that advice, he presented the ointment to King Wu, just as Chuang Tzu reveals the Tao to you through this story.

The Yue Kingdom, the long-standing archenemy of King Wu, is like a long-standing problem in your life. It may be a bad habit you want to break, a dead-end job you want to quit, a codependent relationship you want to end, or any number of other possibilities. You've been stuck with this negative thing in your life, just like King Wu was never able to conquer his enemy.

The ointment changed everything. Suddenly, King Wu possessed a power he never had before. He only needed to make sure every soldier applied it to his hands. In a similar way, the Tao is like a power you never had before. You only have to make sure it is applied to every aspect of life.

The overwhelming victory of King Wu represents the miraculous changes you can achieve with the Tao. The problems you previously regarded as impossible suddenly become easy. Stubborn issues suddenly fall by the wayside. You triumph over your challenges because the Tao has transformed you into a far more effective individual. The challenges haven't changed, but you have.

As the traveler settled in to a life of luxury, the cloth bleacher continued his work, wading into the river each day to make a meager living. He might not be aware of the dramatic changes that had taken place in the state of Yue, and he still could not envision leveraging the ointment for any purpose other than what he knew.

In the same way, there is a gulf between those who play at being Tao philosophers and those who rigorously apply the Tao to life. Modern-day "cloth bleachers," like the frog in the well, are quite secure in their superficial knowledge. Their lives remain stagnant, while those who cultivate the Tao advance toward greater levels of attainment and enjoyment.

The key is skillful actions. The traveler not only regarded the ointment from a new perspective but also took action on his insight. He invested a hundred gold pieces and then sought audience with King Wu. Similarly, once King Wu understood how he could win, he prepared his army, planned strategy, and attacked. The element of action was what transformed the Yue Kingdom into a Wu province, and the traveler into a noble.

Chuang Tzu's message is clear: When tilling the field, it is not enough to turn it over in your mind. Actual work must be done. This work, in alignment with the Tao, need not involve any kind of strife or struggle. It does not have to be difficult if you, like the traveler, can look at it from the Tao perspective and take skillful actions in a creative way.

Ultimately, the choice is yours: Bleach cloth or become a noble. You are the ruler of your own life. You alone have the power to decide for yourself. You can dabble in the Tao and be satisfied at that level. Or, you can wield its transformational power to resolve problems, overcome obstacles, and accelerate your progress.

So . . . how will *you* use the ointment—your own secret formula of the Tao?

PART 2

Travel Advisories

No journey ever goes precisely as planned. Sooner or later, obstacles will come up. There will be delays and detours due to any number of reasons. The road may be blocked off. The weather may turn ugly. We all know this from firsthand experience in the material world—the spiritual journey is no different.

Fortunately, we have travel advisories in the Tao—advanced warnings about the areas of potential trouble, and the alternative routes that will help us get around them. These advisories can help us minimize inconvenience and frustration, as the following:

1. Watch out for turbulence in life. Sometimes, things can get so chaotic that you feel as if you are at the bottom of a huge waterfall, where survival seems impossible. The Tao gives you a way to deal with it so that you will not only survive the experience but even enjoy the process of riding it out.

2. Watch out for the mental blind spot, where you can see the faults in others while remaining blissfully unaware of your own. This is a real risk for everyone, even the most experienced cultivators of the Tao.

3. Watch out for the lure of fame and fortune. Some offers we come across are genuine opportunities, but many more are traps promising position and power, only to deliver disappointment and disaster. When we encounter such temptations, we need to use the Tao to help us stay on the path.

4. Watch out for attachments that become obsessions. Obsessive behaviors are contrary to the Tao and take you far away from your path. Follow Chuang Tzu's advice to take stock of your attachments, so you can prevent them from developing into obsessions. Focus on what really matters in life.

Chaotic Currents

波濤洶湧

Confucius and his students went on a hike in the Liu Liang area, to explore its natural beauty. They saw a waterfall from a distance, so they began walking toward it. They could see that it was huge, and its water fell from such a great height that it splashed down with tremendous force. They could hear a deep rumble and see the mist generated by the splashing torrents.

Confucius remarked: "That water at the bottom of the fall is so powerful and dangerous that not even fish and turtles can get near it. This is all the more interesting because we usually think of water as their native element."

When they got close enough for a better look, they were all surprised by the sight that greeted them. They saw a man in the waterfall being spun around in the ferociously churning water, whipped this way and that by the terrifying currents.

"Quickly, to the rescue!" Confucius commanded. "He must have fallen in by accident, or perhaps he is suicidal. Either way, we must save him."

They ran as fast as they could. A moment later, they arrived at the river downstream from the waterfall. They expected to see the man seriously injured or dead. Instead, they saw him swimming casually away from the waterfall, spreading his long hair out and singing loudly, evidently having a great time. They were dumbfounded.

When he got out of the river, Confucius went to speak with him: "Sir, I thought you must be some sort of supernatural being, but on closer inspection I see you are an ordinary person. How can it be that you were not harmed by the waterfall? Do you possess some special skills?"

"No, I have no special skills whatsoever," the man replied. "I simply follow the nature of the water. That's how I started with it, developed a habit of it, and derived lifelong enjoyment from it."

"This 'follow the nature of the water'—can you elaborate? How exactly does one follow the nature of water?"

"Well . . . I don't really think about it very much. If I had to describe it, I would say that when the powerful torrents twist around me, I turn with them. If a strong current drives me down, I dive alongside it. As I do so, I am fully aware that when we get to the riverbed, the current will reverse course and provide a strong lift upward. When this occurs, I am already anticipating it, so I rise together with it.

Although the water is extremely forceful, it is also a friend that I have gotten to know over the years, so I can sense what it wants to do, and I leverage its flow without trying to manipulate it or impose my will on it."

"How long did it take for you to make all this an integrated part of your life?"

"I really can't say. I was born in this area, so the waterfalls have always been a familiar sight to me. I grew up playing with these powerful currents, so I have always felt comfortable with them. Whatever success I have with water is simply a natural result of my lifelong habit. To be quite frank, I have no idea why this approach works so well. To me, it's just the way life is."

The Tao

This is one of Chuang Tzu's stories featuring Confucius in the central role. It depicts Confucius as a wise teacher and a humble student of the Tao. This may be surprising to those who have been taught that Chuang Tzu often ridiculed and criticized Confucius.

The more we study Chuang Tzu, the more we see that this is just another misconception. A true sage would have no need to ridicule or criticize anyone, and twenty-five hundred years ago there were no such labels as Taoism or Confucianism. What all the masters studied and taught was simply the Tao. These masters, including Chuang Tzu and Confucius, learned from one another with courtesy and mutual respect. It was their students in later generations who started rivalries and strayed far away from the teaching of harmony.

In this story, the majestic waterfall of Liu Liang is the metaphor for life, and the fearsome force of this waterfall is the chaos we all go through from time to time. The water carries so much power that there is nothing one can do to stop it or slow it down. In the same way, we often find ourselves propelled by the progression of events, heading toward a certain outcome and powerless to avoid it. The sheer force of fate, like the waterfall, can be overwhelming.

There are beginners in Tao cultivation who like to say we all live in the Tao and can never be apart from it, so everything is already perfect as it is. With the waterfall story, Chuang Tzu points to a higher level of understanding. While we are indeed immersed in the Tao like fish in water, that water is not necessarily perfect. Because life is dynamic and constantly changing, it can often push us in unexpected directions. In this sense, it is more like a waterfall than a peaceful pond.

Most of us attempt to survive the waterfall of life with limited success. Sometimes the water slams us against rocks or tosses us around like rag dolls. Sometimes we try to fight the water, but the effort is draining. We rail against such injustice, but no amount of rage makes any difference.

Sometimes, like Confucius witnessing the man emerging from the river safe and sound, we see remarkable people who handle life with effortless ease. The mighty current of misfortune does not have the same effect on them as it does on us. They get through the misfortune unharmed and actually seem to be having fun! How can this be?

The man in the waterfall is like a sage who has mastered the art of living life to the point where his skills have become completely natural. Such skills go far beyond "techniques" or "strategies" that one can learn from self-improvement books. They are totally integrated with the sage's instincts and reactions.

There are two major elements in this kind of mastery:

1. *Perceptive Awareness*

   Just as the man in the waterfall follows the nature of the water, the sage is keenly aware of his environment and the forces at work in it. He brings observations and insights to the present moment to understand exactly what is going on. To him, living the Tao is not just about letting go. He is actively interested in his surroundings and curious about current events. This is how he follows the nature of life.

2. *Proactive Involvement*

   Once the sage understands the direction and velocity of a life current, he works with it. Rather than let himself be thrown around by the current, he rides it. Just as the man in the waterfall sees water as a friend, the sage embraces life. Rather than fight the tremendous power of the water, the sage leverages the power for his own purpose.

Some of the currents drive us downward. Such currents represent setbacks in life, and we all encounter them from time to time. The sage's understanding of the Tao informs him that no current can sustain the downward push forever. Sooner or later, it must reach an extreme and turn back around. Those who are able to anticipate this can take advantage of the upward movement; those who cannot may very well miss the opportunity.

How do we become masters of the waterfall, or expert surfers riding the waves of life? Chuang Tzu gives us the following steps:

- *Step 1:* Get to know life and its many currents. Think of life as your friend, not your enemy. When something goes wrong, it is not the result of fate working against you but the result of you not knowing it well enough to work with it. Thus, your best remedy is to get better acquainted.
- *Step 2:* Start practicing with the currents. As you become more familiar with the nature of water, start working with it while remaining observant and sensitive to changing conditions. When the currents change direction or speed, you must adjust yourself to match. The more you do this, the better you will get at it.
- *Step 3:* Make a habit out of this practice. Commit yourself to riding the currents every day, until the skill becomes an integrated part of you. When you get to this point, you no longer have to think about it—you will automatically know the best course of action when you face powerful currents coming at you.
- *Step 4:* Enjoy yourself. Like the man in the story who derived lifelong enjoyment from the waterfall, you will find that dealing with the chaotic currents in life can actually be a lot of fun. It is always interesting and never boring. The challenges it throws at you are never the same.

Enjoyment is the final and most important instruction from Chuang Tzu. Sometimes, people think of the spiritual journey as an ordeal, a trial by fire where one elevates spirituality through hardship. Chuang Tzu tells us this is not the case. The journey may seem challenging at first, but Tao cultivators see it as a dynamic process, so they respond to it with their own dynamism. They enjoy the process, like the man swimming with the currents and having the time of his life. To them, there is no ordeal—life is the ultimate fun ride.

The Mantis Hunts the Cicada

螳螂捕蟬

One day, Chuang Tzu *was walking through the woods near a chestnut orchard. He was enjoying the day and admiring the scenery when he heard a sound from above. He looked up and saw a strange bird flying toward him.*

Chuang Tzu had never seen a bird quite like it before, with such a wide wingspan and huge eyes. He was trying to figure out what to make of it when it dipped low and brushed his head as it flew past, much to his surprise.

"What kind of bird is this?" Chuang Tzu asked himself. "It has such large wings but can't seem to keep itself up in the sky. It has such big eyes but can't seem to see me in its way."

Chuang Tzu took out his slingshot and went after the strange bird. He saw it landing on a chestnut tree, so he approached silently, intending to hunt it down.

As Chuang Tzu got closer, he saw an interesting scene unfolding before him. There was a cicada chirping away in the tree, blissfully unaware of a mantis sneaking up on it, ready to pounce. The mantis itself, totally focused on getting the cicada, was also unaware that the strange bird had just landed close to it and was getting ready to snap it up.

Chuang Tzu saw the irony in the situation. The bird was not aware of Chuang Tzu's approach, just as the mantis was not aware of the bird, and the cicada was not aware of the mantis.

"This is clearly a pattern of the Tao in life," Chuang Tzu thought to himself. "All living things are looking to gain an advantage for themselves, but the process also imposes a burden on them. Generally speaking, the potential gain right in front of you causes you to forget the potential disaster right behind you. The two are connected."

Chuang Tzu targeted the bird and was congratulating himself for his new insight about the Tao when a voice behind him made him jump: "You! What are you doing in my orchard?"

It was the gardener in charge of the chestnut orchard. In going after the bird, Chuang Tzu did not realize he was trespassing into private property. He was so preoccupied that he did not hear the gardener coming up behind him. He dropped his slingshot and made a hasty exit out of the orchard. The gardener, still thinking Chuang Tzu was there to steal chestnuts, continued yelling after him angrily.

This experience had an effect on Chuang Tzu for days. One of his students noticed and asked: "Master, you seem rather unhappy. Is something wrong?"

Chuang Tzu related his experience and sighed. "I was fixated on external appearance and lost sight of the internal essence. Lao Tzu always said that no matter what place you go to or visit, you should always be mindful of the rules of the environment. I forgot all about that when I went into the chestnut orchard."

The student thought about this and said: "Master, that seems like a minor mistake anyone can make."

"The issue goes deeper than that," Chuang Tzu explained. "The cicada, mantis, and bird were all unaware of the danger lurking behind them. This was a great lesson for me, but I did not learn it well enough. I, too, was unaware of the gardener behind me, who thought I was stealing from him. That is why I am unhappy with myself—I can see that I still have a long way to go in cultivating the Tao."

The Tao

To be mindful of where you are is to have situational awareness. Tao cultivators blend in with the environment by observing local laws, customs, and social norms. They go with the flow and draw no attention to themselves, so that they can be comfortable and relaxed in any place, facing any situation.

This insight is not unique to the East. St. Ambrose, one of the most influential figures of the fourth century, was the source of the expression "When in Rome, do as the Romans do." Even though St. Ambrose was separated from Chuang Tzu by thousands of miles and hundreds of years, the wisdom he expressed was the same lesson taught in this story.

Chuang Tzu admitted he was quite human and capable of making mistakes. Although he knew the lesson taught by Lao Tzu, he still fell short when the time came to apply it. This was a powerful reminder that he was still a student, just like everyone else. His reputation as a great teacher made no difference in this regard. His admission of the mistake demonstrated his humility.

As we dig deeper, we uncover more wisdom from the story. Its central image is the hunter who is also the prey, represented by the mantis, the bird, and Chuang Tzu himself. They were so focused on hunting that they did not realize they were also being hunted. In general, being overly attached to something causes you to be blind about your situation, and it is not just about the hunter–prey dynamic. In describing this pattern, Chuang Tzu is pointing to a common failing in all of us.

There are many examples because it is something that happens all the time. Think of all the people who gossip about others, while unaware that they themselves are the subject of other people's gossip. Think of the person who tells others not to judge, while unaware that he is being judgmental. Most of us see what's in front of us, but not what is behind us.

This is why Chuang Tzu described the bird as being strange. Its wingspan meant it should be able to fly high in the sky, and yet it was dipping low. Its large eyes suggested it could see clearly, and yet it could not. This is a way to say that we all have the potential to soar far above the pettiness of mundane bickering, and yet we bring ourselves down to the level of the lowest common denominator. We all have the potential to clearly discern truths and falsehoods, and yet we seem to have blind spots, especially when looking at ourselves.

How can we solve this problem? The answer is in the story. Chuang Tzu has written not only a description of what is wrong with us but also a prescription for the cure. That prescription is the following:

1. *Awareness*

   Simply by being aware of the mental blind spot, we can take a significant step toward not being quite so blind. We all have spiritual eyes that can see clearly, if only we would look through them. Thus, we begin by practicing mindful awareness at all times, on what is in front of us, behind us, and all around us.

2. *Inward Focus*

   When Chuang Tzu fixated on the external appearance, he lost sight of the internal self. The same thing can happen to us, particularly as we become increasingly mired in the sights and sounds of daily life. Thus, we must always remember to turn the gaze inward, to allow ourselves the space and time to reflect on reality. Those who practice this consistently can never be overwhelmed by the illusions of the material world.

3. *Discussions*

   Chuang Tzu ends the story with an exchange between himself and his student. This is his way to point out that we can all benefit from other perspectives. Oftentimes, we find that we can see others more clearly than we can see ourselves. By the same token, others can often see in us problems that have eluded our attention. The best travel companions in your journey are the ones who have your back just as you have theirs. Value your connection with them—cherish your conversations with them. None of us can do it alone. Together, we can do anything.

Do not be the strange bird, flying too low and seeing too little. Listen to Chuang Tzu's words: Soar far above the fray and see clearly. Pay attention not just to the external appearance but also to the internal essence. Look ahead of you even as you remain mindful of what is behind you. Journey safely, free from danger you still have a long way to go.

The Sacrificial Cow

祭祀的牛

A royal envoy *came to a village to look for its most famous resident, Chuang Tzu. When he found the sage, he bowed and said: "Master, I bring greetings from His Majesty, King Wei of the Chu Kingdom. The king is a great admirer of yours and would like to offer you an invitation."*

Chuang Tzu smiled at this, and the envoy continued: "His Majesty has great plans for the kingdom and needs a sage such as yourself as his royal minister. This is a position of tremendous power, Master. You'll live in luxury at the palace, with nothing but the finest clothing and food, and all must bow to you with the greatest respect, because you will represent His Majesty in everything you say and do."

The envoy thought Chuang Tzu would be excited by this offer, but Chuang Tzu did not seem especially impressed. He asked the envoy: "Have you ever seen the cow that is prepared for sacrifice at the annual festival? The peasants drape a beautifully embroidered ceremonial cloth over it and feed it the finest feed, as much as it wants. When they lead it to the temple for the ritual, all villagers in sight kneel down and pray to it. Have you ever seen it?"

This question was so unexpected to the envoy that he could only nod in response. Chuang Tzu then asked: "When the cow is about to be slaughtered for the ritual, do you think it wants to be there? If you were in the cow's position and aware of what will happen, would you not rather exchange places with the calves out in the field?"

"Of course I would, Master."

"Even if that means giving up the finest clothing and food, as well as the respect of the people who bow down to you?"

The envoy finally understood. Chuang Tzu smiled again. "I think you know my answer now. Please convey my gratitude to His Majesty for thinking of me."

The Tao

The first message in this story is a warning against the overzealous pursuit of power. So many of us compete with one another to climb the social ladder, but at what cost?

It is not uncommon to see high achievers who have neglected their health and relationships. Publicly, they may seem like the royal minister, commanding others and enjoying all the good things in life. Privately, they may feel more like the sacrificial cow about to be slaughtered.

The second message in this story is about the temptations we chase after. The blanket to cover the cow represents the material things we desire; the feed for the cow is the physical pleasures we seek; the praying of the villagers is the attention we crave. Chuang Tzu's message is that these seemingly attractive things, carried to an extreme, can lead us down a path of destruction. The festival may be a celebration for the villagers, but for the cow it is the end of the road.

Does this mean Chuang Tzu wants us to refrain from having any kind of material success? Is he teaching us that a life of poverty is a life of happiness, like the carefree happiness of the calves in the field?

No. The Tao is not about poverty. It is about awareness. Being aware means understanding what you are getting into, not just for the present but also for the future. Never be the sacrificial cow, being led around by the nose with no clear idea of what will happen next.

When you encounter a choice in life, it is like coming up to a fork in the road, where you have to choose which way to go. An offer like the position of royal minister is like a path that looks good initially but turns out to be difficult and hazardous. The farther you travel down such a path, the worse it gets. By the time you give up and turn back, you've already wasted too much time and effort.

Not all choices in life are like that. You may receive an offer that is in tune with the Tao. It can be a genuine opportunity that leads to fulfilling work, personal growth, and great benefits for you and others. It is a path that may not seem remarkable at first but turns out to be easy and safe. The farther you travel down this path, the more you enjoy yourself.

Use Tao cultivation to help you choose wisely at the crossroads of life. Bring a higher level of awareness to all the choices you make, and always look beyond the initial impression to perceive the underlying factors. That is how the Tao can warn you against the dangers of the road and show you how to navigate away from hazards. Think of it as the ultimate GPS . . . for the spiritual journey.

The Horse Lover

愛馬的人

Once there was a man *who was obsessed with horses. He spent all his time taking care of them, especially his prized possession—a powerful stallion of tremendous value. He loved this horse so much that he would often use a large wicker basket to catch its droppings and a container made of seashell for its urine. This was because he wished to quickly remove any offending waste from the presence of his beloved steed.*

One day, he was feeding this stallion and grooming it as usual. He heard a buzzing sound and saw that a large fly had landed on the horse. "Trying to feast on the blood of my steed? I'll teach you!" Angrily, he slapped at it on the horse's backside.

The horse, startled by the sudden slap, reacted reflexively. Its massively muscled legs kicked out and struck the man dead center. Such was the force of the kick that the man died instantly. Then, the horse resumed munching on the feed placidly, without any awareness or the least bit of care that it had just killed its owner.

The Tao

The elements in this story are not what they seem. The horse isn't really a horse, but a symbol representing an all-consuming attachment. The horse lover isn't just a character in a story. He is you, me, and everyone else. He stands for all of us when we become obsessed with something.

This sort of obsession has symptoms that can be easily recognized through the following:

- The amount of time we devote to it. Like the horse lover wanting to be around horses all the time, we find that we only have time for the subject of our attachment . . . and nothing else.
- The effort we invest into it. The wicker basket and seashell container were valuable items. The horse lover used them because he wanted nothing but the best for his stallion. When we are in the grips of an obsession, we go all-out in the same way, sparing no expense.

If left unchecked, the obsession will do more than just take up time and effort. It will also take over the mind. You engage in discussions with others about it, make elaborate plans for it, and think about it all the time. Eventually, its needs outweigh your own needs and the needs of your loved ones.

Sometimes there is an unwelcome intrusion into your world, like the fly landing on the horse. If your obsession is a hobby, perhaps the fly is the necessity to break away from it to take care of mundane chores. If your obsession is your work, perhaps the fly is a friend trying to talk to you about the lack of life balance. Whatever the fly is that lands on the horse, you react to it with annoyance, and then anger.

Being annoyed and angry causes you to make mistakes. Perhaps you forget about an important event, or ignore the signs of declining health, or snap at friends and loved ones who are worried about you. You lash out at the intrusion. You slap at the fly.

Then, the horse kicks you. This kick may take the form of a serious health issue like hypertension or cardiovascular disease, or an injury from a hobby-related accident, or a relationship broken beyond repair. Whatever form it takes, it is a devastating blow.

As you suffer the blow, you have to ask yourself one question: You may love the horse, but does the horse love you back? Does it look after you like you look after it? Does it care about you the way you care about it?

The answer is "no" to the above, and this point is underscored in the story by the horse continuing to feed placidly. Your all-consuming attachment is not a person. It cannot love you, look after you, or care for you like a person can. The love and affection you shower upon it goes into a bottomless pit. When you get hurt, your obsession will never notice your pain. When you die, your obsession will never mourn your death. This is why you have to put everything in the proper perspective and make sure the horse does not become more important than the people in your life.

To live with meaning is to have the right focus in life. That focus cannot be obsessions, attachments, or hobbies. It must be people, because the love you put into your personal relationships comes back to you many times over. This is the real message of the story. Never allow yourself to become the horse lover. Follow the Tao to become who you really want to be—the people lover.

PART 3

Travel Tips

Along with the challenges and potential hazards, your journey also offers ample rewards. At every turn, you may take in the breathtaking scenery of divine wisdom or wide-open vistas of the expanded mind. Such wonderful discoveries remind us why we went on the journey in the first place.

To maximize such rewards from the journey, we look to the essential skills in applying the Tao. The more we can navigate through life skillfully, the more we will be able to enjoy the experience. To that end, Chuang Tzu gives us the following tips:

1. Use your ability to observe everything from a detached perspective. Bear witness to the marvelous workings of life and tap into your inner knowing about the world. You may find that you are wiser than you realize when you fully utilize your connection to the Tao.

2. Use your intuition along with your senses to guide yourself through various situations in life. Deal with issues as a whole, and also as parts

to be separated out efficiently. Use this Tao to be at your best, maintain your sharpness, and complete your work with satisfaction.

3. Use hands-on experience to find the optimal balance in everything. Whatever you need to do, there will be the right speed and the right amount of force to give you the best possible results. Keep in mind that this is something you can only learn from life itself—not from books.

4. Use the art of reduction in every aspect of life. The Tao is all about simplicity, so the Tao process is about subtraction rather than addition. Remove obstacles and complexity to unleash the power of your natural capabilities and to fully express your vast potential.

5. Use the Tao of leadership when you interact with others. Chuang Tzu will guide you so you will know what to do when called upon to lead, and what to look for when you wish to identify leaders who are aligned with the Tao.

The Happiness of the Fish

知魚之樂

One day, Chuang Tzu and Hui Tzu took a walk on the bridge arching over the Hao River. At its highest point halfway across, they could look down to see fish swimming in the clear water.

Chuang Tzu sighed and said: "Look how happy the fish are. I envy their happiness!"

Hui Tzu sensed an opportunity to gain an upper hand over his old friend in their ongoing philosophical debate, so he smiled and asked: "You are not a fish. How do you know the fish are happy?"

Chuang Tzu recognized the attack but was unfazed. He shot back: "You are not me. How do you know what is known or unknown to me?"

Hui Tzu had already anticipated this response, so he countered smoothly: "That is correct. I am not you, and therefore I cannot know what is in your mind. By the same reasoning, you are not a fish, and therefore you cannot know what is in the mind of a fish."

Hui Tzu was quite sure this would end their little debate, with himself as the victor, but Chuang Tzu did not look ready to concede. Seeming just as relaxed as ever, he said: "Let us go back to your first question to me. You said, 'How do you know the fish are happy?' You did not ask me if *I knew.* You asked me how *I knew.* That means you already knew that I knew."

Hui Tzu turned Chuang Tzu's unexpected response over and over in his mind but could not frame a rebuttal. Seeing this reaction, Chuang Tzu laughed. The moment was priceless. He said: "I know, my friend, just by standing here above the Hao River."

The Tao

This is one of Chuang Tzu's best-known stories. However, it is not the best understood. Some storytellers tell only the first half, because the second half seems too complex. Some leave out Chuang Tzu's last statement, since they are not sure what point he was making.

At the surface level, this story appears to be a humorous exchange between two scholars. Hui Tzu's perspective was that the only way to know something for sure was to experience it directly. Everything else was speculation. Chuang Tzu was one step ahead. He understood the importance of direct experience. He also understood that there were two ways of knowing that transcended direct experience. This story was constructed to reveal both of them at a deeper level of meaning:

1. *Intuition*

   Intuition was what Chuang Tzu meant when he said "you already knew that I knew." He was pointing out that all human beings know certain things intuitively, even though they may sometimes deny it. We think we should justify and prove what we know, but intuition does not care about justifications or proofs. It leaps over logic for the right answer without bothering with the steps in between. You end up arriving at the truth, but you are not quite sure how you got there.

2. *Observation*

Observation has always been the chosen method of Tao cultivators. Ancient sages realized they could figure out much of the world simply by observing everything with a detached state of mind, and Chuang Tzu described this process using the various elements of the story. The Hao River is the world, and people are the fish swimming in it. The bridge above the river is the elevated perspective of detachment. From there, sages can see how people are glad to be alive, and how they go about their business every day with optimism, like fish swimming merrily.

This method of observation is applicable in all aspects of life. We can, for instance, understand how gravity works by observing its effects, even if we cannot see gravity itself. It is no different with the Tao. Even though the Tao is formless, we can still increase our understanding of it through the power of detached observations.

There is a trap in the study of the Tao, in that students might think not knowing anything is a sign of great wisdom. You may have seen this kind of pretentious sagacity before—perhaps a self-proclaimed guru declares that the more he learns, the less he knows, and since he has learned so much, he knows very little. Thus, his response to any question is: "Who knows?"

Who knows? The Tao answer is *You do*. If you look deeply enough into yourself, you will see that you do know. You know the meaning of beauty and goodness, even as others deny it with the platitude that everything is relative. You know what is right or wrong, good or bad for yourself, even as others try to convince you that such things are illusory. The truth is always there in your heart. Sometimes it can be obscured by the glib distortions of philosophical tricks, but not for long. You can always use intuition and observation to bring out the truth.

When you understand Chuang Tzu's teaching completely, you will find yourself standing above the Hao River alongside the sages. As you look down to observe the world from your detached state of mind, you find that you can see more than you ever thought possible. You see the happiness in the world with crystal clarity, and you know, with great certainty . . . that you know.

The Chef Cuts the Ox

庖丁解牛

Once upon a time *in ancient China, there was a man who worked as the royal chef for Duke Wen Hui. One day, the duke happened to see him cutting up an ox in preparation for dinner.*

There was something about his movements that caught the duke's attention. His hands were gentle and confident as he touched the ox and leaned against it. Even the placement of his feet and knees seemed practiced and assured. He moved in a way that reminded the duke of the Mulberry Woods Dance. As he slashed his blade in and out, it was as if he were playing music, making sounds that never fell out of rhythm.

"Excellent!" the duke exclaimed. Then he asked: "How did you develop your skills to such an advanced level?"

The chef put down his knife to reply: "What I follow is the Tao that goes beyond all skills, Your Highness. When I first started doing this, I saw the ox in its totality, just like most people. After three years, I mastered this process and no longer looked at the ox as an ox. Instead of using my eyes, I used my mind to perceive the animal. My physical senses would be inactive as I reached out with my feelings and directed my mind."

"Interesting." The duke knew he had to hear more. "Go on."

The chef continued: "I follow the natural flow, letting my knife slice through its structure, moving from one large gap between its bones to the next. Its tendons and muscles come apart easily, almost without effort. An average cook goes through one knife a month, because he hacks. A good cook goes through one knife a year, because he cuts. I have used this knife for nineteen years. It has butchered thousands of oxen, but the blade is still as sharp as ever."

"What about the joints? How do you handle them?" the duke asked.

"Your Highness, the joints have openings, which are huge compared to the thinness of the blade. With precise guidance, the knife can swish right through such an opening, with room to spare. That is why my knife still works like new after nineteen years. Of course, I know that joints can be quite complex, so every time I come across them, I make use of caution by focusing my attention and slowing down my movements. Sometimes it takes only one small, exact cut of the knife. The ox comes apart and may not even realize it is dead as it hits the ground."

The duke was impressed. "You certainly seem to enjoy this work," he said to the chef.

"Yes, Your Highness." The chef reflected: "When I'm finished, I survey my handiwork knowing it was a job well done. I put away my knife and feel a profound sense of satisfaction I cannot easily express."

"Excellent." The duke smiled. "The words I have heard from you go beyond cutting up the ox. Today I have learned a priceless principle about living life!"

The Tao

Butchering may seem like an unlikely subject for Chuang Tzu. Is it really the best way for him to express the Tao? Why a messy job like butchering? Why not tell a story about meditation instead?

Chuang Tzu preferred using everyday, down-to-earth examples to explain the Tao. Butchering was one such example. It was something that everyone could understand back in his day. It was also a way for him to express that the Tao was everywhere—not just at the temple but also in the kitchen; not just in meditation but also in mundane activities like meal preparation.

How can we live life the same way? The story offers four guidelines:

1. *Maintain Your Sharpness*

   Many people struggle mightily against problems in life. When they try to force their way through obstacles, it is like an average cook slashing his way through an ox. They may eventually succeed, but only at a great cost their blades get much duller.

   In this context, the sharpness of the blade refers to your physical, mental, and spiritual well-being. When this sharpness is blunted, your well-being suffers, and your ability to handle other problems in life diminishes.

This is why the Tao is so practical. By mastering and practicing the proven methods of the sages, you resolve problems (cut through oxen) effortlessly. You feel no exhaustion, full of energy (your blade remains sharp), and you are ready to face whatever other issues may surface.

2. *Use Your Intuition*

Tao sages never rely solely on their physical senses. Like the chef meeting the ox with his mind, they always look beyond the surface to discern the underlying essence. This is particularly important in life, because so often we encounter situations that are not what they seem at first. Going by the appearance, like seeing the ox with the eyes instead of the mind, will all but guarantee that we miss the hidden agenda.

Once the sages perceive the underlying essence of a situation, they follow the dictates of this essence to determine their actions and words. To them, this is a simple matter of moving along the natural path. To others, they seem to be demonstrating advanced skills.

3. *Focus Your Attention*

Joints represent complicated problems in life. There may be contentious situations where making one side happy will make the other side mad, and vice versa. One cannot solve something like this with a simple solution, just like a blade cannot separate a complex joint with a straight cut.

Sages deal with such problems by focusing their attention. They observe the situation from different perspectives until they see exactly where they can do the most good. Often, this is a pivotal point where the skillful application of leverage produces the greatest impact. When they finally take action, it may be something small—perhaps only a word or a gesture—but the dilemma falls apart, just like the ox.

4. *Create Your Art*

Chuang Tzu's last point is that living life can be an art. Even if you do not think of yourself as an artist, a life well lived can be like a beautiful painting. If butchering can be done with artistic flair, then is there anything that cannot be done in a similar way?

There is a sense of fulfillment when you complete a work of art. It goes beyond the joy of maintaining one's physical, mental, and spiritual health. When you are done, you can put away your tools with a feeling of satisfaction. Everything has worked out exactly as it should, and all is right with the world.

As the duke said, this is a priceless principle. As the royal chef demonstrated, no matter what it is you do, there is always a way to do it that is effective, effortless, and enjoyable at the deepest level. This is the true meaning of *wu wei*.

When your journey in life brings you into contact with another ox, bring out your blade—it should be as sharp as ever, if you have followed the teaching correctly. Regard the ox not with your eyes but with your mind. Let the Tao move your hands, but slow down whenever appropriate and vary your approach until you find the right spot.

Before long, you will become the skillful royal chef. Everyone around you will think you have advanced skills in solving the most difficult problems in life. You alone will know that it is not a skill but the Tao—which goes beyond all skills!

The Wheelmaker

輪扁斲輪

One day, King Huan *was reading a book while an old craftsman was busy mak-ing wheels in his work area. The wheelmaker saw that the king was absorbed in reading and became curious. He put down his tools and approached the king, saying: "Your Highness, what is in this book you are reading?"*

King Huan held up the book with great respect. "The words of sages."

The wheelmaker asked: "Are these sages still alive, Your Highness?"

The king shook his head. "No, they are long gone."

"I see." The wheelmaker nodded. "In that case, Your Highness is reading the leftovers of the ancients."

This struck the king as incredibly insulting. His anger flared. "You are nothing more than a lowly craftsman. Is it your place to comment on what I read? Explain the reasoning of your statement and I may let you live. If you fail to do so, I shall have your head!"

The wheelmaker responded calmly: "Your Highness, I can explain by using what I know about making wheels. The hole in the center of the wheel has to be just right. If I chisel too quickly and make the hole too big, the wheel will slip off the axle. If I chisel too slowly and make the hole too small, the wheel will fit too tightly or won't fit at all. Therefore, the secret of my trade is making the hole just right so the wheel is easy to use and turns well."

King Huan snapped: "What does this have to do with my book?"

The wheelmaker continued: "This skill of making the wheel just right is something I can describe with words but can never pass on to my son. Without years of practice to develop the feeling to guide the work, he will never be able to master my techniques. That is why I am seventy years old and still making wheels. The wisdom of the sages is just like that. Their words are still in the book, but their real essence from years of living the Tao was lost when they passed away. That is why I said the book contained the leftovers of the ancients."

King Huan did not expect such a profound explanation. He set the book down and began to reflect on the wheelmaker's words.

The Tao

One of the first things we learn about the Tao is the importance of moderation. Chuang Tzu makes this point with the wheelmaker's craft. His wheels work best when the center hole for the axle is not too big or too small. We find the same to be true in life—everything is closer to the ideal when we have neither too much nor too little.

This optimal point will not be the same for everyone, just as there is no perfect size for all wheels. Mass production techniques and precision measurements did not exist in ancient China, so the wheelmaker had to customize the fit of each wheel to a particular axle. Life is a lot like that for us. What works well for one person may not work for the next. We have to figure out what is best for ourselves by venturing forth and accumulating experience.

When a wheel fits too tightly, the wheelmaker can always use a hammer to force it onto an axle, but this damages the wheel. It is the same in life, when we try to force something against its nature. For instance, forcing yourself to eat too much damages your body. Similarly, forcing your beliefs onto someone else damages your relationship. The damage may not be easy to spot at first, like tiny cracks in a wooden wheel, but it's just a matter of time before the wheel splits apart.

When a wheel fits too loosely, the wheelmaker can always ignore the problem and try to pass it off as done, but this results in an unsafe chariot. It is the same in life when we are lax in enforcing discipline, especially on ourselves. For instance, we may blame it on traffic when we're late or we may tell ourselves "just one more" when we're trying to quit a bad habit. Everything seems fine, but it's a temporary illusion. The problem is still there, and sooner or later the wheel will slip off the chariot and cause it to crash.

We can also apply the concept of moderation to the process of getting things done. Oftentimes we make the mistake in thinking that faster is better, so we try to work as quickly as possible. We push ourselves to do more in less time, and in the mad rush we make mistakes, forget details, and stress ourselves out.

Chuang Tzu is pointing out that this is not the best way. We should be like the wheelmaker, working in tune with the Tao and sensing the natural pace of the task at hand. This pace is not too fast and not too slow—fast enough to ensure the timeliness of results and yet slow enough to ensure a high level of quality.

A good friend once told me that when she was a little girl, her family would be rushing to get ready for church every Sunday. When her grandmother saw this, she would always say: "Let's slow down so we can get there faster."

This may sound like a paradox but is in fact great wisdom. We are usually going too fast, so slowing down will bring us closer to the right speed. This may not be the fastest speed possible, but it is the best speed for making progress without accidents and other self-inflicted delays.

How do we know what the right speed is? There is no magic formula. The only way to discover the natural rhythm of the Tao is through experience. By living life with awareness, we can sense the most appropriate speed in any situation. It is like the wheelmaker's techniques that could not be passed down to the son in words. Knowing the right speed is something that cannot be taught, but it can be mastered through years of practice.

Chuang Tzu's message for us is not to completely discard books but to put them in their proper place by understanding the limitation of words. Reading a description of how to make wheels can never give you the skills you will gain by actually making them. Similarly, reading a book about the Tao can never give you the wisdom you will gain by actually living life.

This message is especially appropriate for us because we have far more books than were available back in Chuang Tzu's time. Anyone who wishes to read such books has many choices. Beyond books, we also have access to magazines, documentaries, the Internet, and numerous other sources of information. However, we are no wiser than the ancients, despite having so much more than they did. This is precisely the issue Chuang Tzu is pointing out.

Books can be useful as a starting point. They can point the way and provide ideas for us to begin our own exploration. Beyond that beginning, it'll be up to us to apply the chisel to the wheel. We need to experience the process, learn from it, and refine our understanding based on it. This is what yields the life knowledge to balance the book knowledge.

As you read books about the Tao, including this one, always keep the words of the wheelmaker in mind: All books contain leftovers, meaning they are filled with dead, static knowledge, while the Tao is all about the vibrant, dynamic wisdom of life. Thus, if you look for the Tao in books, you won't find it anywhere . . . but if you look for the Tao in life, you will find it everywhere.

Huangdi and the Boy

黃帝與牧童

Huangdi, the legendary *Yellow Emperor, had heard of a sage by the name of Dawei who was known for uncommon insights. He decided to seek the advice of this sage, so he and his six ministers embarked for the Juchi Mountain, where Dawei lived.*

When they neared their destination, they found themselves lost in the wilderness. None of them knew much about the area, so they needed to ask someone for directions. They looked around but could not see anyone.

Huangdi saw a young boy walking a horse not far away. He called out to him and said: "We are heading for the Juchi Mountain. Would you happen to know where that is?"

The boy replied, with a nod: "Sure."

There was something about the boy's straightforward manner that piqued Huangdi's interest. He decided to probe further: "How about the great sage Dawei? Would you happen to know where he lives?"

The boy gave another nod. "Sure."

"What an unusual boy!" Huangdi thought. He seemed so self-assured, like a know-it-all. Was there something he did not know? Half in jest, the Yellow Emperor smiled. "I suppose next you will say you know how to rule the empire, right?"

The boy said: "Ruling the empire is just like taking care of a horse. Why make it more complicated than that? I am just a boy who likes to wander around alone. I had a headache today and felt dizzy, so an elder told me it would help to be out here in the wilderness. I am feeling much better now, so I can continue to be on my way. Governing people is similar to this . . . but, it is not my job, so I should not presume to have an opinion."

"True, it is not your job," Huangdi said. "But before you go—what do you mean by ruling the empire being like taking care of a horse?"

The boy did not respond, so Huangdi asked again. After a thoughtful pause, the boy said: "What is so different about the two activities? When taking care of a horse, what one must do is remove everything that is harmful to the horse in order to bring out the horse's own natural vitality. The way to rule the empire is similar."

Huangdi was stunned. Somehow, what the boy said was exactly what he needed to hear. He bowed three times in gratitude and said: "You are truly a teacher of the heavenly Tao."

Huangdi rejoined his ministers. One of them asked: "Your Majesty, shall we continue our search?"

"No," Huangdi said, to everyone's surprise. He smiled. "I have the advice I need. Let us head back to the palace."

The Tao

Huangdi and his six ministers (Fangming, Changyu, Zhangruo, Xipeng, Kunyan, and Huaji) were all cultivators of the Tao. Later in life, they would all attain a high level of spirituality from their cultivation. Together, they became known as the Seven Sages. At the time of this story, they were still learning, still seeking wisdom.

Chuang Tzu wrote about the emperor as a metaphor for the individual, similar to the way Lao Tzu wrote about the king or the ruler. The emperor had absolute power over his empire, just as you have full control over your inner being. The way for the emperor to govern better is simply the way for you to manage your life more skillfully, in accordance with the Tao.

Huangdi's search for Dawei is similar to our own attempts to look for answers in life. We know we're not living up to our true potential, but what can we do to turn things around? Like Huangdi and his ministers being lost in the wilderness, we're not sure which way to go.

When we have this uncertainty, we tend to try anything, hoping to find the right path by exploring everywhere. This is why people flock to teachers of spirituality and read books on self-improvement techniques. They keep adding knowledge, but this does not necessarily lead to the change they need.

Through the character of the boy, Chuang Tzu shows us the better way. The

Tao does not accumulate or increase complexity—it reduces, simplifies, and streamlines. It's not about learning more techniques—it's about discarding the harmful elements.

When the boy did this for a horse, the horse became healthy and strong. When Huangdi did this for the people, the empire became prosperous and powerful. When you do this for yourself, your life becomes vigorous and vibrant. In every instance, the method is the removal of obstacles to allow the Tao to express itself naturally and completely.

What are the harmful elements you should remove? Everyone is different, but some of the common ones are as follows:

- Habits that are unhealthy or even destructive
- A negative mind-set that leads to frequent complaints
- Tendency to sabotage your own success
- Physical, mental, or spiritual clutter
- Inertia or indecisiveness that prevents effective action

Everyone is different, so you will want to examine your life to identify the harmful elements specific to you. Acknowledge them and write them down for yourself. This is the first essential step to removing them.

Work on the harmful elements one at a time in a subtractive process. Subtract negative influences in your life by creating distance from them. Subtract bad habits by replacing them with good ones that empower you. Subtract malicious, unworthy thoughts by releasing them from your mind. Subtract clutter from your surroundings by donating or discarding them.

The effect of this cultivational work can be dramatic. You will get to a point where you can feel the increase of energy, happiness, and vitality every time you remove a harmful element from your life. You will see that it is more effective than any techniques or "secret" to be found in books.

Huangdi did not actually need the sage in the Juchi Mountain. The only thing he needed was the truth that the boy pointed out. It is the same with you. You do not need to look for answers in the material world. The only thing you need is the Tao that Chuang Tzu has pointed out in this story. There is a power within you, like the vitality of the horse or the might of Huangdi's empire. It is time for you to unleash this power.

The Tao of the Bandit

盗亦有道

Once upon a time *in ancient China, there was a notorious bandit by the name of Zhi who led a group of outlaws. One day, one of his men asked him: "Hey, boss, do we bandits have the Tao?"*

The other bandits thought this might be a joke, but Zhi answered seriously: "Absolutely! How can we not follow the principles of the Tao? In fact, there are five of them that are especially important."

The men all wanted to know what the five principles were, so Zhi listed them one by one:

"A bandit has to be able to figure out where people hide their treasures. This is the principle of insight, being able to see what others cannot.

"*A bandit has to be willing to go into a heavily guarded mansion first. This is the principle of courage, leading the way with bravery and determination.*

"*A bandit also has to be willing to cover everyone's exit by being the last to leave. This is the principle of loyalty, sacrificing one's safety to protect one's fellows.*

"*A bandit has to be able to evaluate a situation in terms of danger, safety, failure, and success. This is the principle of discernment, the ability to think clearly and judge wisely.*

"*Lastly, a bandit has to make sure everyone gets an equal share of the loot. This is the principle of fairness, so no one will be left out.*

"*These five principles—insight, courage, loyalty, discernment, and fairness—are the Tao of the bandit. If you do not have all five, it will be impossible for you to become a great bandit.*"

The Tao

Was Chuang Tzu actually teaching people how to excel as bandits? Not quite. He chose to tell the story this way for dramatic effect and to highlight the universal nature of his message. If the Tao applied even to bandits, then one could be quite certain that it would also apply to all other walks of life.

This story is not just for people who aspire to become great leaders. You can still benefit from it even if you have no such aspirations. The five principles can help you evaluate the leaders you come across, so you can identify the ones that are closest to the Tao.

For example, in the world of business we often see an entrepreneur leading employees, or a manager leading his or her team. Such leaders would use the principles in the following ways:

1. *Insight*
   They must look both further and deeper in order to be insightful. Good business leaders are unconventional thinkers. Sometimes they see reasons to be cautious when others see only a profitable situation to exploit. Other times, they see opportunities where others see only trouble.

2. *Courage*

They must lead by personal example rather than by words. Those who talk more than they do may sometimes succeed as critics, but they will always fail as leaders. They must also take action proactively and be willing to do what they ask of others. Their willingness is what imparts authority to their delegation of tasks.

3. *Loyalty*

They must be the first to offer their loyalty to the team. They understand that a good team takes care of its members so that every person will take good care of the team. Team loyalty is a powerful force in any enterprise. Great leaders understand how to harness this force and build on it.

4. *Discernment*

They must be able to make accurate evaluations and assessments. This is particularly crucial when leading the way through an unstable economy or into a highly competitive marketplace. It's all about knowing the probabilities, the potential payoffs, and where to place one's bets.

5. *Fairness*

They must always be equitable. Nothing destroys a team faster than a leader who plays favorites. A good leader makes sure that everyone does his or her fair share of work, and no one is allowed to slack off. When the team wins, a good leader makes sure everyone benefits equally. No one gets left out.

Zhi was able to succeed as a bandit by following these principles. Similarly, a business leader can do the same and enjoy success at his or her chosen level, from a small business owner to a tycoon or a captain of industry.

The universal nature of the Tao means these are the same five principles we should follow in every aspect of life involving group dynamics, not just in business. Whether you are interacting with family, friends, neighbors, or community, you may find yourself in a situation where people are looking to you for direction—even if you do not wish to take on that responsibility.

Look at the people from the perspective of your journey and it is easy to see that they are your fellow travelers, sharing the same path with you. At the moment, you are ahead of the pack, blazing a trail for them and showing them the way. Think of Zhi the bandit, and use insight, courage, loyalty, discernment, and fairness to guide you into the Tao of leadership.

PART 4

Arrival

Your spiritual journey, like everything else, has a beginning and an end. For those who think of the journey as a sacred task, the end of the journey means completion of the task. For those who think of the journey as a lifetime, the end of the journey would seem to be death itself.

Tao cultivators are a bit different in that they always integrate their lifelong missions into the very fabric of their lives. To them, the two are essentially one and the same. Thus, the end of one's life marks the completion of one's work, and vice versa.

We recognize the significance of the journey's end for many reasons, not the least of which is its connection to death. Mortality has always been a major concern for most human beings throughout history, and most religions of the world attempt to soothe prevalent fears by promising rewards in the hereafter. How about those who study the Tao? How shall we approach death?

This is where we will find Chuang Tzu's wisdom to be particularly important and valuable. He provides us with a series of insights, as follows:

1. Why should we let ourselves be overwhelmed with grief when a loved one passes away? What would happen if we understand that the great circle— life manifesting from the Tao and returning back to it—is no different from the changing of seasons?

2. If we recognize the true inevitability of death, then we know the time will come when we lose those we care about the most. This is a wake-up call that we all need to appreciate one another in the here and now, while we still enjoy the gift of life together.

3. Detachment is the one lesson we all have to master, because none of us will be able to take anything with us when we die. It is not enough to just talk about it. We need to practice it, exemplify it, and live it, so we can depart this world with no concerns and no regrets.

4. What is the underlying reason for us to fear death? Why do we expend so much effort in useless attempts to ward it off? How would we change our thinking if we had even a glimpse into the unknown?

5. Discard the illusion that death is the final destination. See instead the truth that death is the transformation of existence. Your spiritual journey continues on, because you continue on. The end of one particular journey is never the end of all journeys. Thus, the end of this journey is not the end of you. It is simply your arrival.

The Death of Chuang Tzu's Wife

鼓盆而歌

Chuang Tzu's wife *passed away, so his old friend Hui Tzu came for a visit of condolence. When he arrived, he saw that Chuang Tzu was sitting on the ground, drumming on a pot and singing a song. He did not seem to be grieving, and this seemed very inappropriate to Hui Tzu.*

He said to Chuang Tzu: "What are you doing? Your wife has been there for you all these years, raising your children and building your family with you. Now she is gone, but you feel no sadness and shed no tears. You are actually drumming and singing! Isn't this a bit much?"

"It is not what it looks like, my friend." Chuang Tzu faced Hui Tzu's emotions. "Of course I was struck with grief when she passed on. How could I not be? But then, I realized that the life I thought she lost was actually not something she had origi-

nally. During all that time before her birth, she did not possess life, a physical form, or indeed anything at all. She ended up in exactly the same state, so she did not lose anything."

Hui Tzu had to admit this made sense. He had never thought of human life quite this way before.

"Her death was a transformation, just like when she was conceived and born," Chuang Tzu continued. "In that state between existence and nonexistence, her initial transformation gave rise to energy. That energy gave rise to a physical form, and that physical form took on life to become a human being. Now it's the other way around, as her continuing transformation returns her to the Tao. This whole process—from nonexistence to life, from life back to nonexistence again—is like the changing of seasons, all completely in accordance with nature."

Hui Tzu nodded. Somehow, Chuang Tzu's behavior no longer seemed as inappropriate as before. He said to Chuang Tzu: "Since the transformation is perfectly in accordance with nature, it is not something to be sad about, just like you and I would not cry over autumn changing into winter."

"Yes. She is now resting peacefully in the hereafter, without all the constraints and limitations of life. The more I think about that, the more silly it seems for me to cry my eyes out. I will always miss her, but it is not necessary for me to grieve for her as if her death were a great tragedy."

The Tao

This story applies not just to one's spouse, but all loved ones—family, friends, the people we care about the most. When someone like that dies, it is only natural for us to grieve. This grieving process is something that Chuang Tzu experienced and fully acknowledged.

Sometimes, the grief can be so powerful that it overwhelms us. When that happens, everything seems hopeless as we find ourselves completely unable to get on with life. We know such a despairing state is not something the deceased would want for us, but we can't help ourselves.

There is another side to the overwhelming experience of grief, although it can be difficult to discern while we are caught up in it. The death of a loved one is something that forces us to face mortality, to somehow come to terms with it. We can even learn something from it, just as Chuang Tzu did in the story.

What Chuang Tzu learned was the same wisdom attributed to Mark Twain: "I do not fear death. I had been dead for billions and billions of years before I was born, and had not suffered the slightest inconvenience from it."

Whether expressed by an American icon or a Chinese sage, the spiritual truth is one and the same: The life that we think belongs to us is in fact something we borrow temporarily. We must give it back sooner or later, precisely because it is not ours to keep. In essence, this death that we grieve over so much is not that different from our obligation to return books to the library. When the due date comes, we must do our part to keep the system moving along.

Understanding this returning process frees us from debilitating sadness. Chuang Tzu knew that his wife did not just vanish but had simply returned back to nature, back to the Tao. She made the return trip that is really the same trip that brought us here in reverse. Why should we attach excessive emotions to it?

The way that Chuang Tzu explained it is the easiest way to understand. We can look at our journey from the Tao to the material world and back again as transitions and realize that these transitions are perfectly natural, like the changing of seasons. We know that seasons must change when the time is right. We also know that this kind of change keeps going indefinitely. The end of one particular summer is not the end of all summers. We may miss the warm days as we head into cold weather, but we do know that summer will return.

It is just like that with life and death. Some of us have been taught to regard death as the termination point—something to fear, something to avoid thinking about too much. The truth is just the opposite. Death is natural. It is a process of transition and an agent of change that brings spiritual clarity. We don't have to let it overwhelm us. We don't have to fear the Reaper. Instead, we should be inspired by Chuang Tzu to honor the passage of our loved ones, to celebrate the life that they have lived, and to give thanks for the time that they spent with us.

This is the true perspective of the Tao on death. Do not be misled into thinking the Tao is concerned with physical immortality. That is the shallow opinion of dabblers. The truth, as you have heard directly from Chuang Tzu, is deeper and far more interesting.

The Death of Chuang Tzu's Friend

知己難逢

One day, Chuang Tzu *was attending a funeral when he passed by the grave of his old friend Hui Tzu. He turned to his followers and said: "Once there was a carpenter in the Kingdom of Yin who routinely demonstrated an incredible skill. He would dab a bit of lime on his nose, a layer as thin as the wing on a fly. Then, he would ask a stonemason to remove it.*

"Onlookers assumed he meant for the stonemason to wipe it off, so they were all startled when the stonemason brought out a large ax. He would wave it around with practice swings, and everyone could feel the force of the ax like the wind. They could see it was a powerful weapon.

"Then, with the carpenter standing still, perfectly relaxed, the stonemason would swing the ax right in front of him. To the onlookers, it seemed as if the stonemason

had chopped his nose off. In reality, the carpenter would be completely unharmed—and the bit of lime on his nose would be gone.

"When the king of Song heard of this remarkable feat, he had to see it for himself. He summoned the stonemason to his presence and commanded: 'You are the one possessing the special skill, correct? Demonstrate it for me.'

"The stonemason replied: 'Yes, Your Majesty. I have the ability to remove a coating of lime from a man's nose without harming him, but I regret to say I cannot demonstrate it for you. The demonstration will only work if I perform it with my partner.'

"The king said, 'Why did you not say so? We shall simply bring him here.'

"There was a note of infinite sadness in the stonemason's reply to the king: 'That is not possible, Your Majesty. My partner has passed away. I am afraid our special skill . . . is lost forever.'"

Chuang Tzu paused to reflect on the past. After a moment, he said: "Ever since Hui Tzu's death, I've had no opponent for my philosophical debates, and no one to speak with for my discussions. For me, there is also something special that is lost forever."

The Tao

Chuang Tzu was in his twilight years when he told this story. Many of the people he knew had passed away. Even though he regarded their passings as natural occurrences, their departures still left a void in his heart. He could not help but miss them.

The large ax that Chuang Tzu described was a metaphor for communication. Specifically, it was about the words we use when we communicate with each other.

Just as the ax has sharp edges, our words have the potential to cause damage. When we engage each other in conversation, it is as if we are swinging axes around. One wrong move and we wound someone's pride, offend people without meaning to, or criticize someone inadvertently.

Most of the time, we keep our axes covered up for safety. We use politeness and manners to wrap around the sharp edges. This works well in social situations, but sometimes the protective cover gets in the way when we wish to communicate directly and candidly.

The story refers to the performance by the carpenter and the stonemason as a special skill. This is because personal communication is imprecise, so it can be very difficult to get it right. Words mean different things to different people, and the meaning can be further changed by tonality, gestures, and facial expressions. When we think about the many ways misunderstanding can occur, it seems like a miracle that communication works at all. Thus, when we are actually able to understand one another perfectly, it is indeed very special.

You experience this specialness when you spend time with good friends and loved ones. In their presence, you can relax and be yourself. You can speak your mind and rest easy in knowing that you will be completely understood. A soul-to-soul connection is made, and a kind of magic happens. They know what you are thinking, and you know their thoughts. They know what you are going to say, and you can complete their sentences. It's almost telepathic, but there is nothing supernatural about it. It's a plain, simple, everyday miracle.

This kind of miracle has three essential components:

1. *Affinity*
   This is a rare and precious thing that does not arise automatically when you meet someone. For most of us, finding others who are perfectly in tune with us is the exception rather than the rule. When the carpenter passed

away, the stonemason could not find anyone to replace him. In the same way, those who possess a natural affinity with us have a unique role. They are indispensable to us.

2. *Time*

It takes time to really know someone. The stonemason and the carpenter practiced their special skill over many years. In the same way, we need to nurture a relationship over the long haul, with shared experiences and quality time spent together. Natural affinity is a good foundation—but it won't do much good unless we build on it.

3. *Trust*

The third and most important ingredient is trust. Complete, absolute trust is what the special skill is all about. The carpenter knew the stonemason would swing the ax with unfailing accuracy, and the stonemason trusted the carpenter not to make sudden moves to ruin the performance. Both sides must come together.

For us, trust is also the most important ingredient in personal communication. If trust is not present, you can choose every word carefully and still fail to convey your meaning—everything you say is suspect and open to the most negative interpretation, and any attempts to explain or clarify yourself may make the situation even worse.

When trust is present, it trumps everything else. Even when you can't think of the right words or you stutter badly, it doesn't matter. They'll tell you it's okay, because they know what you mean. They know what you are trying to say. Trust makes all the difference in the world.

It is not easy to have all three ingredients come together. Think of someone you know. Do you feel an affinity with him or her? Have you known this person for years? Is there a strong, mutual trust between the two of you? If you can answer "yes" to all three questions for even a few people in your life, then you are truly blessed.

This blessing cannot be taken for granted. As time goes on, your affinity with these special people may fade. You may spend less and less time with them. Something may happen to break the trust between you. Or, as was the case with Chuang Tzu and Hui Tzu, you may lose someone to the passage of time. When the rare and precious miracle is lost, it leaves an emptiness in the heart. We may realize, too late, how wonderful it was when someone filled that void.

This is the ultimate message of this story: Do not wait until it is too late. Consider your good fortune to have these people in your life. Acknowledge your connection with them as the rare and precious gift it is, and cherish the time you spend with them while they are still around. Treasure your performance of the special skill with them and thank them for partnering with you all these years.

They may have no idea what you are talking about, but that's okay. They will sense what you mean and understand what you are trying to say. This simple understanding will demonstrate, yet again, the three ingredients of the miracle—our most incredible miracle of all.

The Death of Chuang Tzu

莊子將死

It was almost time *for Chuang Tzu to pass on. He was on his deathbed, surrounded by his disciples, who informed him that they were making preparations for an elaborate funeral.*

"Why do we need to make things so complicated?" Chuang Tzu asked. "Instead of all these items you are planning to bury with me, I would much prefer having the sun and the moon as my burial jades, and the stars as my jewels. I have the myriad things of the world to accompany me into death. Can't you see that everything has already been prepared for my funeral? Why add anything more to it?"

The senior disciple tried to reason with him: "Master, if you don't want the items, we will have nothing to put in your coffin."

Chuang Tzu remained firm: "I don't want a coffin either. Just leave me out in the open. Heaven and earth shall be my coffin. What can be better than that?"

All the disciples objected: "Master, if we do that, the vultures will come to feed on your body!"

"That's right." Chuang Tzu smiled at them. "If I am aboveground, the vultures will feed on me. So what will happen if I am underground? Well, it shall be the worms and insects that will feast on me instead. Can you give me a good reason why I should favor one over the other?"

The disciples looked at him and at one another, completely at a loss for words. Chuang Tzu looked back at them with amusement in his eyes. This, he thought to himself, was not a bad way to go at all.

The Tao

Chuang Tzu was always the sage who not only talked the talk but also walked the walk. To him, the concept of detachment was not just something to discuss. It was the way he lived. It was also the way he wished to die.

His disciples, on the other hand, still thought in conventional ways and placed much importance on all the considerations of the material world. To them, an elaborate funeral to honor their teacher made sense.

What they failed to comprehend was what Lao Tzu expressed in chapter five of the *Tao Te Ching*:

> *Heaven and Earth are impartial*
> *They regard myriad things as straw dogs*
> *The sages are impartial*
> *They regard people as straw dogs*

The straw dogs were small figurines made from straws, to be used in rituals in ancient times. They were an important part of the ritual while it lasted, but their usefulness ended when the ritual was over. They were summarily dumped in the trash or burned on a pyre without a second thought.

This was Lao Tzu's striking metaphor for life. The physical bodies that you and I inhabit are the straw dogs. While the ritual of life is happening, it is important for us to care for the body, for it is an indispensable part of the ritual. When the ritual of life comes to an end, the straw dog is no longer important or useful, so it is discarded. Seeing this clearly teaches us that there is no need to be overly attached to the body or to anything else.

This was exactly what Chuang Tzu wanted to say, in his own unique way. While his disciples were concerned about what items should accompany him into the hereafter, he alone saw the truth that you literally cannot take anything with you. The more we take this truth to heart, the more ludicrous it will seem to argue about what should and should not be included in the coffin or burial chambers.

Death is the ultimate form of detachment. It is not a trip for which you need to pack and prepare. It is a return to the simplicity of the Tao, and we go back exactly the same way we came—with absolutely nothing.

This is a wisdom that brings spiritual liberation. When you see that there is no need to worry about or obsess over what happens later, you free up tremendous energy to focus on the here and now. This present-moment mindfulness lets you be at your best. Those who can embody this Tao are truly blessed, for when it is time for them to go, they can leave without any regrets. They know, beyond the shadow of a doubt, that they have left nothing undone.

Of all the things Chuang Tzu could talk about on his deathbed, this was the topic he chose, because he recognized the critical importance of death to life. To know how to die is to know how to live. Chuang Tzu's last lesson, quite naturally, was also the most essential of all his teachings on the Tao.

Tears of Fears

麗 姬 之 淚

In the Land of Ai, *there was a princess by the name of Li Ji, the daughter of the general who defended the borders of Ai. She was captured by enemy forces when the Kingdom of Jin invaded and conquered the Land of Ai. Because of her great beauty, she was offered as a bride to the king of Jin.*

Li Ji dreaded the very idea of the marriage. On the day of the wedding, she refused to come out of her room. She kept crying and would not listen to anyone. After many hours of this, she became too exhausted to put up any more resistance. The wedding took place. To the still sobbing Li Ji, everything passed by in a blur.

After an initial period of adjustment, Li Ji grew accustomed to life in the Jin Palace. The king treated her well and kept her in luxuries she had never imagined. Every meal at the Jin Palace was spectacular. Li Ji had never tasted so many delica-

cies, cooked in so many different ways. The royal bed was also a marvel. When Li Ji slept on it, she felt as if she were floating on air.

There was no denying that her new life in the palace was much better than her life prior to the marriage. As Li Ji reflected on the past, she had to admit to herself that all the crying she did at the wedding was quite foolish.

The Tao

This story is not actually about Li Ji or her marriage. It is about Chuang Tzu's metaphors pointing to something deeper: death—our fear of it, and what lies beyond it.

Li Ji's life prior to her marriage is like our mortal existence. Whatever its challenges may be, we've become fairly attached to it. We don't want to let it go.

The wedding is the event of death. For Li Ji, it was the end to her life as an unwed woman. For us, it also seems like the end. Once we're dead, we will no longer be around to see, to feel, to know, or to experience anything. The world moves on without us. What will happen to all the people and things that mean something to us?

These are not cheerful thoughts to contemplate. More so than negative emotions like sadness, anger, and depression, we regard death with fear because it is the great unknown. What lies beyond the veil of death? Heaven? Hell? Limbo? Oblivion? Religions claim to have the answer, but it all depends on faith, and even the faithful cannot always be certain about everything.

The one thing we know with total certainty is that we cannot avoid death. Li Ji's marriage was not optional for her—wedding preparations proceeded regardless of her wishes. In the same way, death is not optional for us. Every day that passes is another day closer to the grave. We understand this intellectually, even as we deny it emotionally.

Although Li Ji was well aware that her wedding was approaching, when the time actually came, she still could not accept it. In the same way, our intellectual understanding of mortality does not lessen our overwhelming urge to stay alive. We struggle against death when it comes for us. We rage against the dying of the light.

Li Ji's tears had no effect whatsoever. The wedding proceeded as planned. The message here is clear: It won't matter how strongly we refuse to go along with death. Eventually, we will surrender and accept it, not necessarily because we've come to terms with it but because we have no choice.

The story does not stop here. It goes on to describe Li Ji adjusting to her new home. This is Chuang Tzu's gentle suggestion that death is not the end. After the physical body stops functioning, the metaphysical self moves on to the realm of pure consciousness. This is the luxurious palace—your new home beyond the mortal plane.

The delicacies of the palace are your rewards in the hereafter. The karma you have created, good or bad, carries over with you as you pass away. If you have accumulated negativities, you will need to deal with the consequences and make amends. If you have lived a positive and meaningful life, then you will enjoy the rewards you have earned. You know there is nothing more delicious than the fruits of your labors.

The royal bed is the state of immaterial existence unencumbered by physical limitations. In the spiritual realm, you enjoy the ultimate lightness of being, because you are not weighed down by a body that can age, weaken, and get sick. It is as if you can float on air.

Li Ji remembered and regretted her struggles in resisting the marriage. This is Chuang Tzu telling us that once we have returned to the Tao, we will look back on our fierce battles against death and realize the foolishness of our ways.

There is no need to wait until after we die to gain this perspective. We can learn to be more enlightened about death now. There is no reason to fear, no reason to resist, and no reason to struggle. Let death follow the natural course of events, and let it be the natural transition to the spiritual realm . . . exactly as it has always been.

The Dream of the Butterfly

莊周夢蝶

One day, *a friend saw Chuang Tzu sitting by himself, deep in thought. He approached to offer a greeting: "What is on your mind, old friend?"*

Chuang Tzu nodded to him and replied: "I am contemplating a question about the transformation of existence."

This piqued the friend's curiosity. He asked: "What brought about such a question?"

"I was out in the field this afternoon and dozed off under a tree," Chuang Tzu said. "I had a vivid dream that I was a butterfly. I had large and beautiful wings, and I flew above the field in any way I wished, feeling so free and full of happiness.

Everything in this dream felt absolutely real in every way. Before long, I forgot that I was ever Chuang Chou.* I was simply the butterfly and nothing else."

Chuang Tzu's friend remarked: "It sounds like a wonderful experience."

"It was, but it had to end sooner or later. When I woke up, I realized that I was myself after all. This is what puzzles me."

"What is so puzzling about that? You had a nice dream, that is all."

"What if I am dreaming right now? I thought I was Chuang Chou who had a dream of being a butterfly. What if I am a butterfly who, at this moment, is having a dream of being Chuang Chou?"

"Well, I can tell you that you are actually yourself, not a butterfly."

Chuang Tzu shook his head. "I am sure there is a difference between Chuang Chou and the butterfly, but there is nothing you can do to help me identify it, since you may be part of my dream. This is the essential question . . . about the transformation of existence."

* In this story, Chuang Tzu referred to himself by his given name, Chuang Chou (Zhuang Zhou). This was because "Chuang Tzu" meant "Master Chuang"—an honorary title used only by others to express respect for him, not for him to refer to himself.

The Tao

Throughout Chinese history, Tao cultivators of every generation agree: Out of all the stories ever told by Chuang Tzu, this is the one that best captures his essence. This story is the reason why the butterfly has come to represent Chuang Tzu in Chinese culture.

Those unfamiliar with the Tao may find this puzzling. What is so special about this story? It seems rather short and simple. Why do people consider it to be important?

The sages have long noted that the world is full of people who talk too much but say too little that is meaningful. The Tao, on the other hand, expresses all possible meanings while saying nothing at all. In order to be closer to the Tao, the sages aspire to convey more meaning using fewer words. This story is a prime example of that. There may not be many words in it, but there is a world of wisdom embedded in them, in the form of two lessons:

1. *Life*

   We've all had vividly real dreams at one time or another. While in such a dream, you do not question its reality, and you react to everything as you normally would. It is only when you wake up that you realize the experience was not real. Whatever fame, wealth, and material goods you may have gained in the dream disappear upon waking. Whatever sadness, anger, and other emotions you may have experienced in the dream dissipate.

Apply the above to life, and Chuang Tzu's meaning becomes clear. We do not question the reality of everyday existence when we are living through it, but what happens when we awaken from this dream called life? What happens to the fame, wealth, and material goods we may have gained? What about all the sadness, anger, and other emotions we have experienced?

Ultimately, everything we associate with real life is not that different from the stuff of dreams. When we understand this, we will realize that there is no need to get so worked up and stressed out over anything. Our attachments in life are illusory, and sooner or later we will wake up without them.

2. *Death*

Chuang Tzu was well aware that the butterfly began as a caterpillar. He knew that the existence of the caterpillar was earthbound, and its activities were centered around consumption. In time, when it had matured enough, it would form itself into a chrysalis. Inside the chrysalis's protective confines, it would prepare itself for the next stage.

Our mortal existence is not so different. We begin life as we know it in the physical plane, bound to the material world. Most of us are immersed in the consumer culture, where most of our energy is spent on consumption. When we reach our twilight years, we become increasingly inactive and withdrawn. When the time comes, we begin to prepare ourselves for the next stage.

A butterfly that emerges from its chrysalis is completely unlike its previous state as a caterpillar. It is as if a car parked in a garage for a month has somehow turned itself into an airplane. Its "before" and "after" states do not seem to be connected, although we know they most certainly are. The metamorphosis from one to the other borders on the miraculous.

This is the ultimate meaning of death for Chuang Tzu. Death is not the end. It is not a sudden cut to nothingness. Rather, it is a process of transformation and emergence. In that process, the spiritual entity that is your true self emerges from the physical shell that is your body. You stand revealed as a being of light, completely unlike your previous state as a being of substance—and yet inextricably linked to it. This, too, is a process that borders on the miraculous.

Now we can see why Chuang Tzu chose the butterfly as the central symbol of his signature story. It's about the metamorphosis, and it's also about the feeling of freedom and happiness that the butterfly inspires in us. That feeling is the essence of our true nature, and it takes away our fears. It tells us that there is no reason for us to be afraid of death, any more than there is reason for the caterpillar to be afraid of becoming the free and joyous butterfly.

This is the greatest wisdom taught by Chuang Tzu, and his greatest gift to you. When you receive this gift, you see life and death through the eyes of the Tao. When loved ones have passed through the transformation, you may miss them, but you will also be glad for them. You know they are finally liberated from the limitations of the material world, and you can see the beauty of what they have become.

One day, it will be time for you to go through the same process yourself. You will embrace it, for you know it is the natural order of things, and it will happen at a time that is appropriate for you. As so many have already done, you too will emerge from your chrysalis. At long last, you will join your loved ones, to fly together . . . through the limitless skies of the Tao.

Farewell

A spiritual journey can take on many forms. It can be a lifetime, from birth to death. It can be a worthwhile endeavor, from conception to completion. Now, as you turn toward the last page, you see that it can also be your reading of this book, from cover to cover.

Thank you for having embarked on this journey with me. You and I took flight together, on the wings of the Peng bird. We listened to Chuang Tzu together, to heed his warnings and tips about the trip. Now we are on the final leg of the journey, gliding toward the final approach. What will happen after we land, when there are no more pages to turn?

One of the most important things we have learned is that the end of a journey is not the end of all journeys. Therefore, the end of our time together is also not the end of your spiritual quest. As long as you are willing, there are more excursions for you:

THE TAO OF JOY EVERY DAY

365 Days of Tao Living

This is a yearlong journey, traveling at the speed of one page per day. That one page may not seem like much, but it can set the tone for the entire day, so you can be immersed in the Tao as you go through it. Over time, this practice transforms you gradually into a Tao-centric individual. It is the easiest way to cultivate spirituality for those who simply can't find the time for such pursuits.

THE TAO OF SUCCESS

The Five Ancient Rings of Destiny

This is a journey of self-exploration, starting from your innermost spiritual core and expanding outward to your mind, your relationships, your world, and ultimately your destiny. The ancients defined success not in terms of material wealth but in terms of becoming the best version of yourself in every possible way. This is the map that will show you how to get there.

THE TAO OF DAILY LIFE

The Mysteries of the Orient Revealed
The Joys of Harmony Found
The Path to Enlightenment Illuminated

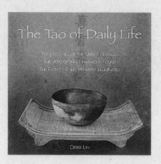

This is the book that started the journey for me. It is a tour of Eastern teachings, with explanations on how to apply the wisdom for Western readers. Whether you are at home, at work, or in social settings, this book can serve as your guide, to point out the potential obstacles you can avoid and the important things in life that you should cherish.

These books are one way to continue your exploration. Another way is through the World Wide Web. The online resources I offer can all be accessed from my Web site: DerekLin.com. Whenever you are ready to embark on your next trip, simply look for me in the departure lounge of the Internet, or the boarding gate of a bookstore. You'll find me waiting there, passport in hand, bags all packed—and ready to accompany you anywhere.

About the Author

Derek Lin is the award-winning author of *The Tao of Daily Life* and *The Tao of Success*. He was born in Taiwan and grew up with native fluency in both Chinese and English. This background lets him convey Eastern teachings to Western readers in a way that is clear, simple, and authentic.

Lin has utilized his linguistic skills to create a *Tao Te Ching* translation that has been lauded by critics as setting a new standard for accuracy and faithfully capturing the lyrical beauty of the original. He is an active speaker and educator on the *Tao Te Ching* and the Tao in general. More information about his work is available at DerekLin.com.